A Cross-Cultural Investigation of Person-Centred Therapy in Pakistan and Great Britain

A Cross-Cultural Investigation of Person-Centred Therapy in Pakistan and Great Britain

Saeed Ahmed Khan

authorHOUSE®

AuthorHouse™ UK Ltd.
1663 Liberty Drive
Bloomington, IN 47403 USA
www.authorhouse.co.uk
Phone: 0800.197.4150

Published by AuthorHouse   01/16/2014

ISBN: 978-1-4918-8916-9 (sc)
ISBN: 978-1-4918-8915-2 (hc)
ISBN: 978-1-4918-8917-6 (e)

Contents

ACKNOWLEDGEMENTS

Firstly I would like to give thanks to my venerable supervisors Dr. Marilyn Hackney and Dr. Nicholas Lund who helped me complete this dissertation. I will always remember their support in enhancing my research skills, writing the dissertation and acquiring knowledge of psychology.

I appreciate the endeavours of my friends especially Bev Denial, and Atarad who led me to seek material useful for the completion of the dissertation.

I am particularly grateful to Dr. Brian Thorne and Dr. Stephen Palmer who gave me information.

I thank my friends in Pakistan who provided me with relevant material.

Finally I would like to thank my parents, brothers, sister, and sisters in law, nieces and my cute nephew who have love in their hearts for me.

CHAPTER ONE

INTRODUCTION

This dissertation is a library-based research project about person-centred therapy in Pakistan and Great Britain. The dissertation is a cross-cultural investigation that seeks to provide information about why, where and how client-centred therapy is used in Pakistan and Great Britain. A great number of psychologists, clinical psychologists, and counsellors use different psychotherapies to deal with people who are suffering from mental disorders. In the modern period, especially in Europe, client-centred therapy is the focus of the counsellor's attention. A number of investigations into this type of therapy have been conducted and still are being conducted.

The term 'culture' has a variety of meanings: nationality, skin colour, country of birth, a shared language, mode of relationships, religion, rituals, warmth, etc. (Laungani, 2004). People interpret the word 'culture' from their own subjective, idiosyncratic, and individual perspectives. Culture can be described in historical terms. It can be called a historically created system of beliefs, attitudes, values and behaviours of people who are bound by a shared language and religion, over a given geographical region. These factors permit people to live in that society so that they build their lives in accordance with the sets of norms established within it. These factors also permit people to organize their collective and individual lives (Laungani, 2004).

People are born into a family that has its own specific history. By the process of socialization people learn how to acquire and internalize language, religion and religious practices, rules and regulations, customs, beliefs, values, and modes of proper conduct that family members and members of the community make efforts to instil in them. People learn a lot from the norms which are prevalent in their society. They learn to understand the differences between right and wrong, good and bad, proper and improper, beautiful and ugly, acceptable and unacceptable, etc. Family is considered a microcosm of a wider part of the community in which people live and reach the stage of their full development. Society gives people a structure that runs their lives, builds their beliefs and practices, and people are able to develop a sense of their selves, of their own lives.

People want to look at society in real terms because it is a combination of groups of people occupy a given territory and live together. Variations in people, even within society, are seen. As people try to make sense of their society they observe that the differences spread over social, economic, political, physical, and other domains of their environment. In spite of this, people are inclined to experience a sense of belongingness, and they have a feeling of 'oneness' with the various groups around them. This takes place when they ascertain that all various groups in their society are unified by a set of core values—religious, aesthetic, political, legal, nationalistic, and social—which form an integral part of their culture (Laungani, 2004).

Anthropologists describe culture as the total of accomplishments and activities of any particular period and group of humans (Triandis, 1980). Therefore culture is considered an abstract concept, an overarching symbolic configuration that is formulated by people in society. It absorbs all the distinguishing human forms of adjustment and the particular ways in which various human populations make arrangements and organize their lives on earth (Levine, 1973). All cultures have a symbolical link with their societies. Although the two are not similar, one cannot understand a society devoid of culture, or a culture without a society (Carrithers 1992; Parekh, 200). Cultures create, grow, change, and in a few cases diminish and might even die or become outmoded (e.g. the ancient Hellenic culture).

A few new specialist areas such as psychological anthropology, cognitive anthropology, and cultural psychology have appeared in recent years (Munroe and Munroe, 1980). There is disagreement within psychology as to how culture should be defined and conceptualized (Laungani, 2004). Triandis (1980) describes how societies face variations by means of their ecology, their survival system, their socio-cultural system, their individual system and their inter-individual system.

There is a shared belief among scholars that almost all cultures of the world have similarities. In other words, it can be said that all human beings have many common universal, behavioural, attitudinal and emotional characteristics. At the same time, every society or every culture retains its own typical features that change alongside many imperative aspects, such as climate, technological development, levels of education, politics, social, economic and environmental conditions, beliefs, attitudes and value systems. Value systems hold an important relation of a kind of factors, consisting of patterns of socialization, development of identities, social and familial arrangements and the beliefs of religion and practices of people in that society (Kakar, 1992).

Several attitudes, beliefs and behaviours (both private and public) of people seem to be culture-specific. Hence, one might expect to find, both within and between cultures, similarities and differences in conduct that define a variety of problems such as health, ailment, mental illness, grief, and bereavement, patterns of infant rearing and socialization, relationships and actuation of identity. All these problems are conceptualised by the people of a culture. It is obvious that one might intend to explore or see differences and similarities in values and behaviours of people of different cultures. Objective knowledge of such similarities and differences can have an important value to psychotherapists, health workers, educators and counsellors, who would be interested in how and why these similarities and differences arise.

The effects of cultures on counselling and psychotherapy cannot be underrated. In Laungani's (2004; 23-25) words: "To ignore the problem of a lack of a single theoretical framework for counselling in relation to culture or to deny its salience is dangerous. To continue to operate with 'free for all' therapeutic strategies may eventually tarnish the image of this noble profession, and lead to a state of epistemological anarchy".

It is very important for therapists from all over the world to discover ways that are suitable for dealing with the complex issues related to culture and psychotherapy. It is said that all human beings have a kind of common biological need concerning their psychological survival. But it is clear that all human beings have differences in many aspects, for example how they see themselves, how they see their private lives and the outside world around them, how they differentiate between wrong and right (Laungani, 2004). The reality is that when one thinks of his/her problems thoroughly, it seems that human beings are recognised by their differences rather than their similarities. When we try to relate differences in attitudes, beliefs and values to people from different cultures, those differences become prominent. What seems unreasonable and inappropriate behaviour to a person of one culture may seem perfectly reasonable and appropriate to a person who belongs to another culture.

This dissertation is a study of cultural differences between two countries, Pakistan and Great Britain. The study attempts to explore cultural differences in terms of counselling settings in both countries. Moreover, the study tries to link person-centred therapy with cultural differences. In short, the study tries to see whether this therapy is useful for problems related to cultural differences.

The dissertation includes five chapters. Chapter One contains the introduction and discusses techniques of person-centred therapy and its use in both countries. Chapter Two shows 'Aims and objectives' of the research. Chapter Three provides information about counselling courses which are taught at universities in Pakistan and Great Britain. In addition, a comparison of these courses has been made. Chapter Four explores the differences which distinguish Pakistani culture from British culture. The study of cultural differences provides information on the usefulness of person-centred therapy in counselling settings in the two countries. Chapter Five is the last chapter of the dissertation, containing the conclusion and recommendations. References are given at the end.

The first chapter of the dissertation will provide a short history of person-centred therapy and its techniques, which are used in therapy sessions. Furthermore, information is given about the use of Person-centred therapy in Pakistan. The main objective of the research into the use of the therapy in Pakistan is to give information about the status of the therapy, and its scope in the field of psychology in Pakistan. In addition, the research indicates a few reasons why person-centred therapy is used less in Pakistan.

"It seems to me that at bottom each person is asking, "Who am I really?" How can I get in touch with this real self, underlying all my surface behaviour? How can I become myself?"" (Nelson-Jones, 2001: 78).

Carl Rogers was the pioneer of person-client centred therapy. This therapy was developed during the period of the 1930s and 1940s. The main objective of this therapy was to help clients fulfil their unique potential and become their own persons. In addition, in this therapy, the task of the counsellor is to guide the client to make contact with his/her inner resources. In 1974, Rogers and his colleagues changed the name of the therapy and gave it the new name "person-centred therapy" (Nelson-Jones, 2001). In person-centred therapy the counsellor establishes full involvement to make a relationship with the client. Person-client therapy is a part of humanistic psychology. The person-centred approach views a person as a social, constructive, and creative being.

"In Rogers' words (1951) the human being has one basic tendency and striving—to actualize, maintain and enhance the experiencing organism" (Merry, 2002: 21). The actualizing tendency, in the person-centred approach, is a single motivation for human development and behaviour. It emerges from circumstances in which a person lives. In addition, it subsumes an impulse that leads to creativity, learning, and the embellishment of the individual. According to Rogers when the actualizing tendency is subject to damage by environmental factors or by abandonment of social obligations, then psychological disorders start forming (Merry, 2002).

Roger says that experiences, sensations, and perceptions form a unique reality. Little by little, a part of our experiencing grows in to a "self-concept." The process of developing a "self" is an action of actualising tendency (Merry, 2002).

In others words, the growth of the "self" develops by interacting with the environment and people with whom a person wants to establish relationships. Originally, self-concept is developed by self-experience and incidents, which occur in an astonishing domain which the individual discriminates as "I" me or "self." After the development of self a person needs to pass through experience of love and acceptance from important people (like parents). In other words, he/she needs positive regards at the same time. A person needs a positive self-regard—a sense of trust in the accuracy and readability of his/her own inner experiencing. Positive self-regard is not strong. It is susceptible to the negative evaluation of others. For the maintenance of self regard, a person has to pay no attention to many aspects of his/her own inner experiencing because if a person does not do this he/she has more chances to lose love and safety at a time when he/she needs it the most. With the passage of time, persons learn to view themselves as others view them, paying no attention to their inner experience whenever they feel that it might be in conflict with values of people who are valuable for them or on whom they want to be dependent. A person learns from experience that he/she is only acceptable as long as he/she thinks, feels and behaves in ways that are positively valued by others. The values, which are based on other evaluations rather than on the individuals own organismic valuing process, are called conditions of worth (Merry, 2002).

"Conditions of worth are prevalent because all too often individuals are culturally conditioned, rewarded, reinforced, for behaviours that are in fact perversions of the natural direction of the unitary actualizing tendency" (Roger, 1977: 247).

Rogers says that self-actualization whose base is an organismic valuing process displays its inimitable actualizing tendency (Nelson-Jones, 2001).

Nelson-Jones says that Rogers gives importance to the parents of a child. He says that greater the degree of unconditional positive regard that parents experience towards the child, the fewer the conditions of worth in the child and the higher the level of its psychological adjustment (Nelson-Jones, 2001: 88).

Rogers says that most people largely interject their values and keep them as fixed conception. They rarely examine and test them. As a result, their level of self-regard is lowered and they are not able to prize themselves completely. In addition, by the process of internalizing conditions of worth, they internalize a process that makes them the agents of lowering their own level of self-regard or of self-oppression.

In development of self-concept, Rogers emphasizes the relationship between partners (whether marital or otherwise). This relationship has growth-inducing properties, which finish conditions of worth and increase the level of self-regard. Rogers also gave his attention to educational institutions, which create emotional climates for the development of healthy self-concepts. He shows his interest in the favour of significant experiential learning that is self-initiated and shows the concerns of students rather than those of teachers or administrators. Furthermore, he emphasised the politics of interpersonal and intergroup relationship that is a more democratic sharing of power and control (Rogers, 1977).

Person-centred theory is a theory of human information processing or of the processing of experiences into perceptions. This process plays a great part for those who are disturbed and face problems of conditions of worth. Rogers believes that when experiences take place in people's lives, their perception of experience could be deformed to solve the conflict between self-concept and experiencing. People with low functioning have their self-concept with conditions of worth that precipitate them to misinterpret while people with high functioning perceive their experiences accurately because they have fewer conditions of worth. When a person becomes successful in symbolizing experiences accurately, there is the self-concept then state of congruence between self-concept, and experience exists. A state of incongruence occurs between self-concept and experience when experience is prohibited and misinterpreted. This state of incongruence could exist whether experience is positive or negative. Clients who come for counselling and therapy have low self-concept and they often refuse and misinterpret positive feedback they get from outside and even stop positive feelings which come from within (Nelson-Jones,2001).

Rogers introduced the concept of subception or pre-perception. Subception provides protection to self-concept when self-conception receives a threat from its current structure. "Anxiety is a state of uneasiness or tension which is the response of the organism to the subception that a discrepancy or incongruence between self-concept and experience may enter perception or awareness, thus forcing a change in the currently prevailing self-concept." (Nelson-Jones,2001: 91). People with low self-concept misinterpret the perception of their important sensory and visceral experiences. Nevertheless, if an important experience takes place suddenly in a high incongruence, the process of defence might not be able to work properly. Thus, anxiety not only exists but the process of defence becomes unsuccessful. The self-concept is very important to people because they need to obtain an accurate perception of themselves and the ways they use to interact with life to fulfil their necessities. People whose self-concepts are effective perceive their experiences correctly (Nelson-Jones, 2001). Person-centred therapy can be described by its two goals: first, the goal of client in therapy and second overall goals reflect the human potential for growth.

The process of person-centred therapy rests on the client's trust in using his or her ability to actualize his or her human potential. In the beginning of therapy the therapist urges the client to understand responsibility for the contents that the therapist will be a good listener to whatever the client wants to share with therapist. No formal assessment is made in person-centred therapy because it is considered that clients do not have stability of their actualising tendency because of their conditions of worth. The therapist helps the client express, experience and explore feelings whether they are positive, negative, ambivalent, or confused. In sessions of therapy the client starts by showing thoughts, feelings, and actions. The therapist asks the client, "Where would you like to start today"? The therapist tries to provide a growth-promoting climate in therapy.

Person-centred therapy is a process in which the thoughts and feelings of both the client and his/her therapist are involved. Person-centred therapy shows clarity of how the therapist considers the client's self-alienation and how he helps him/her to remove problems. The person-centred therapist provides the attitudinal conditions that take away the emotional deprivations which the client experiences. Rogers regarded congruence, unconditional positive regard and empathy as the attitudinal conditions that make the start of therapeutic growth (Nelson-Jones, 2001).

Genuineness, realness, openness, transparency, and presence are the words which are used for congruence. Congruence is the most basic of the attitudinal conditions. Therapist and client are in person-to-person contact. The therapist provides the right growth-promoting emotional climate and the client becomes less defensive and looks for external regard. A mutuality of congruence develops in therapy sessions between therapist and client. This process makes it easier for both therapist and client to be real in the relationship. As a result, the client not only becomes more congruent in therapy sessions but also in his/her outside relationships.

Unconditional positive regard involves the therapist's willingness for clients to be whatever immediate feeling is going on—confusion, resentment, fear, anger, courage, love or pride. (Nelson-Jones, 2001: 99-100).

Rogers emphasized the attitude of the therapist in therapy sessions as to whether it is significant and worthwhile for the client or not. Caring, acceptance, respect, and non-possessive warmth are terms which are used for unconditional positive regard. For unconditional positive regard the therapist trusts in the client's capacities because it is important for constructive change that the right nurturing conditions are provided. If clients try to be smarter, less defensive, and less vulnerable then the therapist will not show positive regard for clients. In addition, there are several restrictions on expressing unconditional positive regard; for example, if a client physically threatens a therapist then the therapist will not give any unconditional positive regard to client.

"Unconditional positive regard is an attitude that is moved forward by clients if they are prized for their humanity and experience an emotional climate of safety and freedom, in which they can show feelings and relate events without losing the therapist's acceptance"(Nelson-Jones,2001: 100).

Empathy is a process in which a therapist is desirous to know and receive the client's communications and meanings. Rogers wrote "To sense the client's private world as if it were your own, but without ever losing the "as if" quality—this is empathy" (Rogers, 1957: 99).

There are several ways for the therapist to be emphatic with the client. The therapist needs to understand the subjective worlds of clients. The therapist has to be sensitive to the flow of experiencing that goes on between the client and him or herself. It is easier for clients to be empathic to themselves both inside and outside of therapy because of the three attitudinal conditions provided by the therapist in the therapy session. The client's self-concept brings his/her experiencing into awareness. Furthermore, the client learns the importance of his/her feelings and considers them a guide to his/her actions and future directions.

A number of critics made criticism on Roger's work from the very beginning. The position of person-centred therapists looks low in the field of academic psychology (Thorne, 2003). In Great Britain well-established training programmes and professional groupings show the professional identity of person-centred therapists in the present time. However, the person-centred viewpoint does not seem to become associated with the spirit of the age. Rogers was criticised throughout his career in two detrimental ways: ineffective and effective (Thorne, 2003).

Geiser (1997) writes that most of the Rogers' theoretical concepts have been modified in everyday language which has weakened the ideas and principles of this approach and has created the basic misunderstanding that client-centred therapy is what everyone does at the beginning of a therapeutic relationship and the real therapy exists after it. Eckert (cited in Geiser, 1997) points out that any link of interpersonal skills, which the therapist uses in therapy, and the result of therapeutic effectiveness cannot be found out but it just seems that it is an effect of therapist who is completely familiarized with Person-centred philosophy. Thorne (1992; 45) says "The core conditions become established not because of what the therapist does but as a result of the attitudes the therapist holds towards his or her client. [In short] client-centred therapists may differ widely in therapeutic style despite the fact that they all subscribe to the same beliefs about human beings and the desirable characteristics of therapeutic relationship".

Keleman (1986) writes that a few therapeutic circles brood over the illusion that the organism comprehends what is best for it. But that is often not true. An organism just understands what is best for it in a field of responsiveness. Rogers (cited in Geiser, 1997) says "This is not to say, however that the client-centred therapist responds only to the obvious in the phenomenal world of his client. If that were so, it is doubtful that any movement would ensue in therapy. Indeed, there would be no therapy. Instead, the client-centred therapist aims to dip from the pool of implicit meanings just at the edge of the client's awareness".

Rogers writes that if psychological conditions go in favour of human beings, they can naturally make progress to get fulfilment of their innate potential. According to Freud (1962) men and women are 'savage beasts', and only the process and structure of civilization can tame their aggressive and erratic sexuality. Further he writes that the instinctual drives of individuals force them to get the self-satisfaction of basic needs. Freud emphasizes the unconscious that is a powerful destructive element and supports the procedure of getting satisfaction. Therefore, a great number of analytical theorists say that Rogers' view of human nature is not only guileless but also misguides because it does not do justice to the unconscious that analytical practitioners consider a determinant that settles perception of reality and behaviour of an individual (Thorne,2003).

Thorne (2003) points out that Rogers' theory presents an optimistic perception of human potential and it underestimates the forces of the unconscious and of evil. Classical behaviourists write that Rogers gave less attention to the relationship between cognitive process and dysfunctional behaviour. The cognitive behaviour therapists see Rogers as a complete 'laissez-faire' and consider that he gave much attention to the feelings and the emotional climate of therapeutic relationship.

Vitz (1994) writes that the theory of human nature Rogers developed presents psychology as a religion in which much importance is given to self worship. Thorne (2003) writes that many criticisms have been made on Rogers' way of 'doing therapy'. One of these issues is related to the therapist's behaviour. Van (1980) describes that the therapist's behaviour can produce a situation in which the client experiences confusion. The therapist's behaviour makes the client dependant rather than autonomous.

As Thorne (2003:79) writes "the validity of the therapeutic relationship in client-centred therapy is deeply suspect in the eyes of many analytical practitioners, who see Rogers' neglect of transference process as an omission with far-reaching consequences."

Masson (1989) writes that the client-centred therapist cannot offer a real 'genuiness' in the relationship. The client-centred therapist creates an artificial therapy situation that helps the therapist play out the core conditions for brief periods.

Watson (1984:40) writes "After twenty-five years of research on Rogers' hypotheses, there is not yet research of the rigor required for drawing conclusions about the validity of this important theory."

In Asian countries, this therapy is used in both clinical and counselling settings but most clinical psychologists are interested in using behaviour therapy, cognitive behaviour therapy, the psychodynamic model, etc. However, person-centred therapy is less used in clinical and counselling settings in some countries in Asia such as Pakistan. The problem in practicing client-centred therapy is that there is no specialist in this counselling approach. In clinical and counselling settings, Pakistan is facing a lack of experts in this approach. A study shows that in Pakistan the ratio for trained clinical psychologists with a minimum of a 12 month post-Master's diploma is approximately 1:400,000 where as the ratio of Psychiatrists is 1:600,000 (Steven et al, 2004: 246).

There could be many cultural factors: poverty, low level of education, lack of awareness of psychological treatment, unhealthy attitude of psychologists and counsellors to clients, and collective-self concept, etc. can all play a great role in less use of client-centred therapy in Pakistan. The limitation of this approach on the Pakistani population is that it deals more with the feelings and demands of self-growth as part of the awareness process during a therapeutic and counselling session, which requires some psychological awareness and intellect, but because of the lack of awareness/exposure, the level of psychological awareness in Pakistani people is not very high. Only 44% of the population in Pakistan is literate and 67% of the population lives in the rural areas where psychological services are not available (Population Census Organization, Statistics Division, 2000). Even among the educated, there remains very little awareness about nonmedical approaches to the treatment of psychological disorders (Steven. et al, 2004: 246). That is the reason client-centred therapy (CCT) may not be solely used and may not be very effective in Pakistan.

Studies on client-centred therapy in Great Britain show what it was used for. Lsatuke et al (2005) conducted research to assess how different processes bring about their respective outcomes in one case of client-centred therapy and one of cognitive behaviour therapy (CBT). On the basis of assimilation analysis of both therapies, the study showed that the client with CCT sessions learned to accept her needs more while the client with CBT sessions managed her needs better.

This dissertation will attempt to describe those cultural differences which have great importance in the use of person-centred therapy and counselling in both countries.

This research would guide students who are interested in using person-centred therapy in Asian countries to cultural differences, which they can make solid ground for further study and investigation of person-centred therapy. Moreover, the investigation will provide information of counsellors' methods of using this therapy in English culture.

The next chapter of the dissertation gives information about why the researcher is interested in this project. In Chapter Two the aims and objectives of doing the present investigation are presented.

CHAPTER TWO

AIMS AND OBJECTIVES

In this second part of the dissertation, the aims and objectives of the research have been described.

The aims and objectives of writing the dissertation are related to factors which stop clients contacting psychologists or counsellors to take psychotherapy sessions in the professional settings of counselling in Pakistan. Factors involved are: lack of awareness of psychotherapy among people in Pakistan, long duration of the therapy process, the economic status of clients, low level of education, patients' frequent visits to doctors rather than psychologists or counsellors, giving preference to medicine rather than psychotherapy sessions, fear of being stigmatized as a mental patient, etc.

Furthermore, it was observed that many psychologists do not use person-centred therapy in their professional practice in Pakistan but rely on behaviour therapies. The reason is that they are trained in behaviour therapies.

The research also draws on observations of British culture. Keeping the factors in mind that are cause of less use of person-centred therapy in professional practice in Pakistan, the decision was made to study cultural differences in the counselling process in both Pakistan and Great Britain. The aims of this study are:

To assess training of person-centred therapy in two countries: Pakistan and Great Britain. For the assessment of person-centred therapy in both countries, training centres were requested to send information about training procedures, in the form of syllabi, leaflets, etc.

To explain cultural differences in counselling in the two countries. For explanation of the cultural differences in the counselling process, a great number of books on Pakistani culture have been consulted. In addition, journals, magazines, and articles have been used. Similarly, books, journals etc. have been used to gather information about British culture.

After the completion of the research, the researcher hopes to achieve the following objectives:

Study of the use of person-centred therapy in two countries. This study will provide information about 'Does a layman have knowledge of this therapy?' and 'Do people like to visit a counsellor or a psychotherapist to get therapy sessions for removal of their psychological problems?' This study will help gather information about the application of person-centred therapy in different areas of life of people in both countries. Moreover, it will give information about the therapist's professional attitude with clients, and the kind of environment that is created in therapy sessions. Furthermore, this study will help to provide knowledge of the client's role in therapy.

Studying the causes which lead to any differences in the use of person-centred therapy in the two countries. This study will show causes that precipitate the use of person-centred therapy in both countries. In addition, the study will discuss differences which distinguish use of this therapy in two countries.

Comparison of the syllabi of counselling training courses in the two countries. Comparison of courses will give information about training programmes which are the main part of the professional counselling setting in both countries. Moreover, comparison of courses will provide information of universities in which theoretical and training courses of counselling are taught.

The next chapter (Chapter Three) of the dissertation contains a comparison of Pakistani and British counselling courses, which are taught in universities in both countries. In addition, the researcher has given some information about the establishment of counselling in Pakistan.

CHAPTER THREE

COMPARISON OF PAKISTANI & BRITISH COUNSELLING COURSES

This part of the dissertation aims to make a comparison of counselling courses taught at British universities and universities in Pakistan. The major objective of the third part of the dissertation is to explore the use of person-centred therapy in counselling courses which are taught to postgraduate students. For comparison, Masters courses in counselling, which are accredited by the British Psychological Society and British Association of Counselling and Psychotherapy, have been chosen and counselling courses which are part of the Master's degree in psychology in universities in Pakistan have been selected.

Counselling is presented by using different labels. People who practise counselling are given different occupational names such as counselling psychologist, mental health counsellor, marriage counsellor, student counsellor etc. All these people get special training in their particular field to make general practice of counselling. A number of agencies and social workers have grown to fulfil the needs of people who pass through traumatic experiences and social problems. These organisations and agencies render counselling in several areas such as marital breakdown, rape, and bereavement. The role of counsellors in these agencies is visible when social problems arise. For example, changing social perceptions of marriage, redefinitions of male and female roles, new patterns of marriage and family life, and legislation making divorce more available represent major social and cultural changes of the past century. Counselling gives a way of assisting persons to work out these changing social and cultural prospects. (McLeod, 2003).

For the last 20 years, person-centred therapy has influenced a number of different fields including education, management, international peace work and cross-cultural communication. In America, Europe and other parts of the world client-centred therapy day by day is drawing the attention of counsellors and psychotherapists to itself (Thorne, B. Mearns, D, 1988). In Asian countries such as Pakistan behaviour therapy, cognitive behaviour therapy, gestalt therapy, and psychodynamic therapy etc., form the major part of psychological treatment, and are currently practiced more than person-client centred therapy.

After many years of development of Clinical Psychology, a large number of psychologists, psychotherapists and clinical psychologists have thought of establishing counselling psychology in practical fields. A study was conducted to propose a comprehensive counsellor preparation model within the philosophical and religious beliefs in Pakistan. The main purpose of this model is to provide a cohesive and comprehensive body of knowledge to counsellors to work in educational, business, health and community settings. This model reflects the philosophy, beliefs, and values of the country in terms of human development, life/ career, and educational planning. In addition, this model proposes a pre-service preparation to replace the current in-service preparation model for counsellors (Almas, I. & F. A . Ibrahim, 1985). Although counselling psychology is taught at Master's level in universities, it requires the support of counselling psychologists to be part of practice. At universities, few students are trained in behavioural therapy, cognitive behavioural thrapy, and psychodynamic therapies for clinical practice.

There is a lack of expertise on the part of clinicians to practice person-centred therapy in Pakistan. A study shows that in Pakistan the ratio of trained clinical psychologists with a minimum of a 12 month post Master's diploma is approximately 1:400,000 whereas the ratio of psychiatrists is 1:600,000 (Steven. et al, 2004: 246). Usually, psychologists working in clinical settings are trained in cognitive behaviour therapy. They prefer applying these therapies. Because of cultural reasons, expectations of quick response, reassurance of end of problem, and medication for solution of their problems, usually clients look up to the doctors and psychologists and they would not feel comfortable if they were asked to just talk about their problems to come to some solutions (Jabeen, 2007).

In many cultures, treatment expectations are different and in these cultures the therapist is taken as an authority and is expected to be directive, to give suggestions and reassurance. For example, Abad, Ramos, & Boyce, (1974) conducted research on Puerto Rican patients and found that patients had expectations of their doctors to be active and concrete in prescribing medications. Following a traditional psychological approach, in which the client is expected to discuss and reflect on problems while the therapist assumes a more passive role, may result in the Puerto Rican client prematurely terminating treatment (Matsumoto & Juang, 2004:373-374). Moreover, the principles of behaviour therapy and rational emotive behaviour therapy are readily understood by the therapist and are a comparatively easy way to treat patients for quick outcomes in therapy, whereas person-centred therapy requires a very sound theoretical background as well as much developed behavioural attributes on the part of therapist. For these reasons, a professional is also reluctant to adopt person-centred therapy as a specialization for their career. (Farhat, 2007).

The trend has changed over the last few years in Pakistan regarding the role of psychologists. Initially clinical psychologists used to work only in hospital settings and treat patients with severe psychological problems and those on medication. Patients who visited the hospitals were those who were suffering from psychotic disorders and would prefer to be treated by medication, as mostly they could not afford the cost of psychotherapy. Hospitals providing psychological facilities are only located in major cities; people usually do not seek help except medication. The overall literacy rate is low. 40% of the population in Pakistan is literate, (Population Census Organization, Statistics Division, 2000), and awareness of psychological treatment is lacking.

Now the trend in schools, colleges and universities is moving towards counselling, especially career and school counselling. Guidance and counselling services in the educational and vocational domains emerged as a result of the efforts of the Pakistan Federation of University Women and other organizations (both national and international). The educational and vocational guidance and counselling movement is on the brink of becoming a national reality at all educational levels (Ibrahim, A, F & Almas, I, 1983). Counsellors are focusing on CCT; the students are educated and more aware of counsellors' therapeutic methods so it is easy to use CCT in schools. Some clinical psychologists with well-educated and insightful clients are also using CCT. The major population catered for with the CCT approach in Pakistan is still the student population.

A large numbers of studies have been conducted on different areas of psychology in Pakistan. At university level in Pakistan students of Masters, MPhil and PhD degrees are trained to work in their areas of interest. Psychology is drawing attention to itself in Pakistan. A few years ago, people did not have exact knowledge of mental disorders; however, with the passage of time, psychologists continued their work on psychopathologies and raised awareness of mental diseases. In this regard, clinical psychologists performed an important role to draw attention to psychology, psychopathologies, and their remedy. Psychologists and clinical psychologists were appointed in hospitals and rehabilitation centres to deal with people who come with different psychological disorders.

In universities, students interested in psychology are taken every year for training in clinical psychology. Counselling and guidance, as an optional subject, is taught to Masters classes. People who are trained in clinical psychology work as clinical psychologists in hospitals and rehabilitation centres. Many of them prefer private practice; one thing common in their practice is the eclectic use of techniques including behaviour therapy, cognitive behaviour therapy. Different therapies are taught to students who intend to work as psychologists but the majority of trainees prefer cognitive behaviour therapy, behavioural therapy, psychodynamic, rational emotive behaviour therapy, etc. Person-centred therapy is taught but students show less interest in using this therapy. Even clinical psychologists make less use of this therapy in their professional practice.

The researcher is interested in working on person-centred therapy in the perspective of Pakistan and Great Britain. The literature review carried out for this research shows that there is a lack of counsellors in Pakistan. For many years, there were no counselling centres in Pakistan. Counselling and guidance is taught in universities as an optional subject. Students prefer studying clinical psychology to studying counselling. Person-centred therapy is not only a part of syllabi of clinical psychology but also it is taught in counselling psychology.

Bearing these points in mind, researcher decided to work on person-centred therapy in the perspective of Pakistani culture and British culture. Furthermore, the researcher would view counselling in both countries by means of cultural differences.

In Pakistan, there is neither any organisation for professional development of counselling psychology nor counselling psychologists (to the best knowledge of the researcher). There exists an organisation that is known as the 'Pakistan Psychological Association' in Pakistan. A great number of professional psychologists, psychotherapists, and clinical psychologists are members of the association.

Most members of the association are clinical psychologists and those who earned their Master's degree in psychology and work as lecturers in different colleges and universities. In professional settings in Pakistan, clinical psychologists and psychologists play a dual role. They not only provide their services as clinical psychologists but also work as counsellors. No societies of counselling psychologists have been established in Pakistan (to the best knowledge of the researcher). In universities, counselling psychology is taught as an optional subject to postgraduate students of psychology while in Great Britain the British Psychological Society and British Association of Counselling and Psychotherapy accredit professional courses. For comparison of counselling courses, some renowned universities in Pakistan which offer Master's degrees in psychology have been consulted. These universities exert some control over colleges in their own areas.

Counselling courses in universities in Pakistan:

University	Degree	Subject	Counselling courses
University of the Punjab, Lahore	MSc	Applied Psychology	1-Introduction 2-Assessment 3-Tests 4-Theories including person-centred therapy 5-Counselling reports
National institute Of Psychology, Islamabad	MSc	Psychology	Counselling is not taught
University of Peshawar	MSc	Psychology	Counselling is not taught
Institute of Professional Psychology, Bahria University	MSc	Psychology Educational Group Organizational Group	Counselling is restricted to organization No CCT is taught
University of Balochistan	MSc	Psychology	1-Introduction 2-Tests 3-Counselling theories including CCT 4-No special training in CCT
Bahu-din Zakria University, Multan	MSc	Psychology	1-introduction 2-Assesment 3-Counselling Approaches 4-CCT No training 5-Report writing
Faisalabad University	MSc	Psychology	1-Introduction 2-Theories 3-Tests 4-Report writing

A review of counselling courses in universities in Pakistan shows that almost every university is running postgraduate academic programmes in psychology in which counselling is taken as an optional subject. In counselling, emphasis is given to 'nature' of counselling, techniques of counselling, theories, tests and submission of counselling reports. No practical importance is given to person-centred therapy. Recently the CPPD counselling School in London has founded a new branch in Karachi, Pakistan. This institute offers a 'Diploma in counselling skills.' In history of Pakistan, it is the first international institute of counselling. Except for this institute, there is no training centre in Pakistan for counselling (at time of writing the thesis).

In Great Britain, a number of universities present courses which have been accreted by the British Psychological society and the British Association of Counselling and Psychotherapy.

Counselling courses in universities in Great Britain:

University	Degree	Subject	Counselling courses
City University London	MSc	Counselling Psychology	1-Theories (including CCT) and their practice 2-Research methods

Regent's College	MA	Psychotherapy and Counselling	1-Theories 2-Training 3-Research methods 4-Dissertation
Roehampton University London	MSc	Counselling and Psychotherapy	1-client centred Counselling 2-Phenomenology 3-Psychotherapy and counselling 4-Research methods 5-Dissertation
University of East London	MA	Counselling and Psychotherapy	1-Practical skills 2-case studies 3-Therapy essay 4-Therapy practice 5-Dissertation
University of Wolverhampton	MSc	Counselling Theory	1-Cognitive behavioural approaches 2-Humanistic approaches 3-Research methods
University of Chester	MSc	Counselling Studies	1-Counselling theories 2-Contemporary Counselling issues 3-counselling skills 4-Psychotherapeutic Practice 5-Research methods
University of Derby	MA	Counselling in Professional Development	1-Counselling Psychology and Practice 2-Theories of Counselling skills 3-Research methods

The major difference in counselling courses taught at universities in Pakistan and Great Britain is that no association/society of counselling psychologists is available in Pakistan to accredit counselling courses. Every university has its own separate syllabi that are issued to different colleges affiliated with universities. Counselling is an optional subject in courses of MSc in psychology. No universities in Pakistan offer a special Masters degree in counselling psychology. The predominant courses are history of counselling, nature of counselling, interview in counselling and interview techniques, tests in counselling, theories of counselling, report writing (so called because students are not interested in counselling, they prefer studying clinical psychology that is a compulsory subject). Almost every university follows an annual examination system. Recently a few universities have started following a semester system but those are non-official universities. Person-centred therapy is taught but no special training is provided to students. The main reason for this is that no counselling psychologist is available, mainly, teachers who earned their simple Masters degree in psychology teach counselling courses or clinical psychology. Research methods are not part of counselling courses. In brief no special courses or training in counselling are available in Pakistan.

In Great Britain, the British Psychological Society, and the British Association for Counselling and Psychotherapy accredit courses in counselling. Several universities offer Masters degrees in counselling psychology. These universities follow a semester system for examination. Seminars, group discussion, presentations, assignments, practical work, individual work, and dissertations are considered the most important part of study. Research methods in counselling, cognitive behavioural skills in counselling, theories of counselling, implication of counselling in different areas of life are part of the counselling course. In short, it can be said that universities in Great Britain emphasize creativity, critical skills, enhancement of professional skills, and research in counselling.

The next chapter (Chapter Four) of the dissertation provides information about cultural differences and problems which could be the result of those differences. Further, the researcher has tried to link person-centred therapy with the differences discussed in the next chapter.

CHAPTER FOUR

EXPLANATION/CULTURAL RESOURCES FOR DIFFERENCES IN COUNSELLING

In this chapter, the fourth part of the dissertation, the researcher aims to identify cultural differences that distinguish British culture from Asian culture. The investigation attempts to explore psychological problems and problems of cultural issues that exist in British society because of cultural differences, and for which people visit counselling psychologists or therapists to remove or get over their problems. Furthermore, the researcher has tried to make a connection between person-centred therapy and cultural differences, which create a great number of psychological and physical problems.

Counselling made rapid progress during the twentieth century (McLeod, 2003). It comprises a number of themes, emphases on practice, and schools of thought. It is not only a process between two individuals but also a social institution that is set in the culture of modern and industrialized societies. It is called a profession, or discipline, that is related to a new creation (McLeod, 2003). Counselling is a process in which a trained counsellor makes a professional relationship with a client. The relationship the counsellor establishes in the counselling process is normally between two persons but sometimes more than two individuals are involved. It helps clients to conceive the views of their lives. In addition, this therapeutic relationship enables clients to attain their self-determined objectives by making meaningful, well-informed choices and by solving problems of an emotional or interpersonal nature (Burks & Stefflre, 1979).

In the 1960s and 1970s, the counselling and psychotherapy community discussed racism and equality and made some strategies for providing knowledge of cultural issues into counselling training and practice. This period provided firm and promotional work of 'cross-cultural', 'transcultural' and 'intercultural' approaches to counselling and psychotherapy, taking cultural aspects into mainstream practice. Knowledge of cultural differences brought up issues to establish an approach to counselling that places the concept of 'culture' (McLeod, 2003).

This approach was given the new name "Multicultural approach." Pederson (1991) says that to be a member of a culture has influence on the development of a person and his/her personal recognition, emotional and behavioural problems—when a person comes to counselling he/she shows how relationships, morality and a sense of 'a good life' are assimilated and interpreted in the culture in which the individual spends his/her life. Furthermore, he says that a strong impression of social and cultural variations affects a society.

The acute form of the impact precipitates a lot of disturbance and a great number of mental disorders. Counsellors, who practice counselling or therapy with minority groups or with people of the same background should have information about the ways of life of people who are in a minority and people who are from the same background. Ignorance of cultural background, expectations of the client and misunderstanding may result in a conflict (Pederson, 1987). If a minority cultural pattern passes through variations with the dominant culture's time frame, it will face problems. Burnham (1986) explains hurdles in time-related cultural patterns. He says, for instance, law directs a few of our rights, such as it is a rule for children to start going to school at the age of 5 years. Other cultural forces however, such as marriage and leaving home could shape others'. In addition, he sums up that "such events signal cultural-specific rules."(p.38)

The great importance for counsellors is to know various practices used in fostering a child and establishment of the family life (Laungani, 1999). Abel Smith and Brown (1996) describe that writings on mid-life matters for diverse cultural groups, for instance, is scattered. "This is significant given the advancing social demographic trend. Namely, a whole new ethnically diverse generation will soon be at the age where retirement becomes a major life transition (Laungani, 1999: 8). For the last twenty to thirty years, interest in diversity-sensitive counselling and therapy has been increasing. It has focused on differences, which include culture, race, gender, sexual and affectionate orientation, disability, religion, socioeconomic status, and mixtures of these among others (Weinrach, 1998, cited in Nelson-Jones, 2001).

All human beings have some universal biological and psychological needs that are important to their biological and psychological survival (Laungani, 2004). Human beings are considered different from one another in many aspects of life especially in terms of how they look at themselves, how they observe their own private world and the outside world, how they differentiate wrong and right, good and bad etc. Human beings can be divided by their differences than their similarities. When we meet and observe people from different cultures, the differences they have in their attitudes, behaviours, and beliefs accentuate them (Laungani,2004). Triands (1994) writes that the prevalent values in our culture influence what we conceive as bad and good, wrong and right, improper and proper. Laungani (1995) writes that normative hopes and values accentuate social and individual conduct. They develop the foundations of familial, social, religious, legal, and political order. Our values are the result of our past religious and philosophical heritages. In the sense of our values and beliefs, and our lives over centuries, we are all captives of our own culture.

Laungani (2004) describes four main cultural differences which distinguish British culture (and Western culture in general) from Indian, Pakistani culture (and Eastern culture in general) in counselling and psychotherapy. According to Laungani (2004) in Asian culture there is an emphasis on collectivism, determinism, emotionalism, and spiritualism. On the other side, there is an emphasis on individualism, cognitivism, free will, and materialism in British culture. Asian and Western cultures are distinguished by different characteristics. However, these are individualism and collectivism, which have drawn the attention of psychologists to cross-cultural research (Cohen & Nisbatt, 1994; Triandis, 1994). The researcher notes another cultural difference in the form of confessionism, and Tawbah (Repentance). Tawbah is a process in Asian culture to get forgiveness from God for sin or wrongdoing (Rizvi, 1989).

Individualism means a third dimension of national culture. It is the opposite of collectivitism. It gives information of relationship of the individual and the collectivity which exists in a given society (Hofstede, 2001). Its reflection is seen in nuclear families, extended families, or tribes. In a few cultures, individualism is considered a blessing and a source of well-being while in some other cultures it is seen as estranged. When thought is given to a broad range of human societies, traditions and modernism, a great number of differences can be recognized in sociability by looking at differences in the complexity of the family system in which people live and the effects of that on their day—to-day behaviour. A few people live in a nuclear family system and some like an extended family system to live in and some still live in tribal units which are based on consanguinity obligations of an even more distant nature (Hofstede, 2001). The relationship between the individual and collectivity in human society not only concerns the matter of living together but also makes a link with societal norms. It not only influences mental programming of people but also affects the structure and functioning of a number of institutions other than family.

In Western culture, there has been an emphasis on Individualism. Individualism has its prominent values in current Western society. It is a separate system from non-Western societies, which emphasize collectivism. The concept of individualism in Western society is taken in different meanings. It is an ability to control one's life. It is an ability to get over one's problems/difficulties. It is an ability that leads to betterment. It is an ability that accomplishes one's internal resources (Laungani, 2004). Layard (2005) writes that the main factors which stop people from attaining happiness and harmonious social relationships are those concerning competitive individualism.

Albert Camus (1955) describes that individualism takes people to existential loneliness. Furthermore, he writes that giving importance to self-reliance, being unable to make adjustment with others in society, and having expectations to get over one's difficulties and problems, bring severe stress for the individual and could make the search for one's identity a lifelong quest. For the last few years, awareness of stress has led to its many remedial programmes. Stress is taken from the phenomenological perspective to explore how people gauge the factors, which are known as stressors, in their lives. Triandis and Gelfand (1998) wrote that collectivism and individualism can be differentiated according to the vertical and horizontal organization of societies, providing four cultural syndromes. These four have their own strengths and weaknesses. Where members of a society tolerate hierarchical relations, it is called a vertical society, while members of horizontal society give preference to equality. A demerit of horizontal individualism is social isolation, because individuals could end up following their own objectives in the absence of main social support for their efforts.

Societies which are known as vertical individualistic societies create emphasis on inequality and competition that could make for high levels of creativity and greater effort, but a negative consequence of those societies is stress, and in the case of failure of competition, depression. The person-centred approach is known as one of the major therapeutic models because a lot of material has been written on it. Clarke (1994) writes in his article that the person-centred approach presents a therapeutic atmosphere because a client is considered in it as fundamentally reliable and valuable. Further, he writes that a person-centred therapist looks for the client's meaning of stresses which the client perceives or experiences. Moreover, he describes that an individual who comes to a therapist for a dialogue suffers from some forms of stress. The most relevant task of the therapist is to establish a therapeutic climate in which client perceives whether he/she is being rewarded or not. The therapist presents a trusting relationship of equality to the client. In this process the client is seen as capable person, through his/her own inherent actualizing capability. So, the person-centred therapist does not provide a ready-made, magical cure or to direct the client towards following any specific coping strategies. This approach gives evidence of how stress-induced ailment could be considered as 'challenges to the sense of identity and meaning that often accompany physical distress' (Barnard, 1984, cited in Clarke, 1994). The person-centred therapist is committed to fulfilling the client's exceptional resources of self-healing.

The ideology of individualism creates its own problems. One is related to "Identity problem." In Western society, 'identity' is taken in socio-psycho-cognitive developmental terms (Laungani, 2004). According to Erikson (1963), identity procedure begins in infancy and faces many critical stages before reaching adulthood. To attain a proper identity that makes a person separate from others, which shows true inner being, and which enables one to fulfil his/her potential, is not easy. This, most of the time, results in the forming of a conflict. If it remains unresolved then it creates stress and in a great many cases, it precipitates identity crisis (Rogers, 1961). Russell (1999) writes that increasing and rapid variations in the social setup of modernity create crises of self/identity.

Cultural and social contexts are changing; therefore, the setup in which identity is formulated is disintegrated.

Therefore, there is a loss of social identity and loss of individual identity. The establishment of counselling and its employment as a social practice is recognized as a modern trend accessory with the establishment of and appearance of the modernist notion of self. Foucault (1998) says that counselling has certainly established its own structure of the self. Counsellors not only present preconceived notions of the self, but also they present a process through which they enable individuals to create their very identity.

In an individualistic society, identity plays a big role in the development of uniqueness of a person and his/her personal and psychological adjustment in the society in which he/she lives. As Erikson (1968) describes, an identity is a construction of individual uniqueness that seeks for continuity of experience and group solidarity. He writes that psychological adjustment of a person rests on his/her personal identity, his/her reference group orientation, and commitment to a particular group. Identity is a core matter for people of minority groups in colonial systems. It is not only a social issue but also a political issue. "Counsellors need to understand the psychological correlates of accepting an identity that has been conferred rather than being self-constructed (Laungani, 1999: 10)". Writings on postmodernism show that identity could be elected, and multidimensionality and fluidity of identities are known as a new phenomenon. It is accepted as the social norm in societies which have a core of multiple ethnic and religious identities.

The rate of identity bewilderment is higher among the indigenous young people reared on a diet of rationalist certainties of modernism and very inclined to the feeling of being alone in a culture much imbued with individualism and privacy. Hoare (1991) writes that persons live within a society that secures and sponsors identity "within a culturally determined relativistically unique cosmology" making a person able to act, live and function naturally and adaptively to the respective cultural context. Kitayama(1997) says that culture plays a crucial role in determining the identity of an individual. The individual gets a sense of identity from the culture in which he/she exists.

A new identity that is a result of intermarriage could be an important issue of recognition in an individualistic society. In other words, mixed race is an issue in an individualistic society. Gilroy (1993) tried to give the idea of a new individual identity of being Black Atlantic for the African-Caribbean people who are intermarrying with the white British population. For children of diverse origin, the experience of becoming a black identity is a more important aspect of their recognition than skin colour. Mixed race is an issue that has drawn the attention of counsellors and psychotherapists in the Western world to the idea that gender and ethnic identification of people of mixed parentage is more complicated than that of children who are brought up in monocultural families (Eleftheriadou, cited in Laungani, 1999)'. Mixed race children frequently face the same degree of inequality as ethnic minority groups. The various differences of inequality rest on their racial composition (Eleftheriadou, 1997). Few studies have been conducted and little literature is available on mixed racial or cultural parentage and the involvement of the formation of their identity. The available research has shown that mixed parentage affects their identity negatively but Tizard and Phoenix (1989) sampled 58 young people aged 15-16 years in their study. One group of children was of one parent who was white and one who was either black African or African-Caribbean. The results of the study showed that half of the group understood themselves as 'black' and the other perceived themselves as 'coloured', 'brown' or 'half and half'. The interesting point of this study was that none of them considered themselves as 'white', though they knew that they had a white part. Nearly two-thirds of them had been positive that they were of a mixed race, but they seemed to have had a more negative perception when younger. Another interesting point of the study was that half of them were desirous to be white when they were much younger. It was also observed that they had experienced more problems than either black or white groups. Factors which performed a great role in the development of their identity were parental attitudes to their mixed race, relationship with their parents, social class backgrounds, school environment, racism, and societal perceptions. The social position of mixed race people is important for apprehension of their needs, adoption, and information of psychotherapy practice (Eleftheriadou, 1997).

Jardines, (1996) writes that the endeavours of combined identity could be strongest in the process of transracial adoption. In addition, he explains that becoming part of one racial group on the side and another taking our group on the inside, such individuals could be unable to voice their concerns about racism, they are not able to associate their racial self and have a sense of being a stranger in that group. Jardines requests counsellors to consider the cultural background of such clients and admit their experience of racism. Luthra et al (1999) writes that "Racism awareness training does not, however, enjoy a good reputation. If not handled sensitively, it can become a form of reverse racism, individually blaming white trainees who are made to feel personal guilt and responsibility for racism in society. The inevitable result is either disempowering of the trainee or a hardening or retrograde movement to a hidden racist position. Consequently, victims of such inept training become defensive. Ultimately this leads to political corrections" (Luthra et al in Laungani, 999:12). The responsibility of how and when to bring up matters of racism rests with the counsellors, not with the client. Mahtani et al (1989) reckon that it is not possible for transcultural counselling to redress racism and poverty. A positive view of antiracism appears in their work and they maintain that their position on culture is not neutral. They admit the ethnocentricity of a great number of practitioners and say that counselling should be provided to all cultural groups.

Laungani (2004) writes that the most prominent aspect of individualism is an identification and honour of a person's physical and psychological space. People often avoid touching one another because it is considered an intrusion of one's physically limited boundaries. Physical contact especially when two males hold their hands in public places is taken to mean homosexuality. Prohibitions of physical touch are very powerful; even in the situation of grief, they cannot be broken. In some situations, people avoid making eye contact. A number of studies have shown that invading another person's physical space leads to extreme stress and to neurotic disorders (Greenberg et al, 1977). Close to the concept of physical space is that of 'psychological space'. It defines boundaries which detach the psychological self from others. This is a view of values, which is honoured in all social situations in the West. Laungani, (1999) reckons that the concept of physical space and psychological space is combined with the concept of privacy. Privacy is about respecting and recognizing the individuality of others. Spielberger & Web, (1979, 1978) say that a number of studies have showed that interference in the privacy of others becomes a cause of severe stress and neurosis and other psychological disorders. Individualism has had an effect on the size of the British family structure.

Bonnnerhea, (1982) writes that the British family structure has gone through a dramatic variation during the post-war period. Variations in the size and the structure of families with high levels of social and occupational mobility precipitate a sense of loss of community life, especially in big cities.

Person centred therapy seems to fit well in an individualistic society because there is an emphasis on individual self in this society. Markus & Kitayama (1997) describe that individualistic construal of self is an independent, and a separate entity that is more common in Western culture. The person-centred approach posits that all psychological problems are the results of blockage of self-actualization (Nelson-Jones, 2001). According to Rogers if clients are given an opportunity in therapy session to express their concerns in their own words, and the therapist does not interfere, they will almost always talk about themselves (Throne, 2003). Nelson-Jones (2001) writes that the task of person-centred therapy is to release the blockage of self-actualization.

In contrast to the individualistic inclination of Western cultures, Asian people are inclined towards the collectivistic

(Sue, 1990). The identity of an individual has a close link to his/her social group in a collectivistic culture, therefore the basic objective of the person is not to maintain independence from others, but to promote the interests of the group (Davidson, Jaccard, Triandis, Morales & Diaz Gurerrero,1976). Hui & Triandis (1986) write that collectivistic culture makes the person's relationships strong who gives less importance to his/her personal needs than to the good of the group or whose objectives do not threaten group harmony. Pakistani and Indian societies are considered as family based and community centred (Sharma, 2002). Mainly, Pakistanis and Indians are fostered in an extended family setup. The father is the head of the family. The family normally consists of all children, the unmarried sons and daughters, married sons and their children, and relatives of the father such as father's younger brother, his children and father's widowed sister. They all live in a joint family system. Income in this family system is spent on all members according to the needs of members. Family and group are considered more important than an individual is. Owing to this, Asians are more harmonized within the social environment and the responses of others (Sue, 1990). This family system, called the communal and caste related system, affects all family members, for example if any member of a family faces physical ailment, psychological or psychiatric disorders or financial problems, this affects the entire family.

In this family system, the individuality and ego of a person are completely covered in the collective ego and individuality of the family and community. People within a group are categorized in caste and sub caste. In the community people are given ranks; elders are given special status, and their role is considered very important and is clearly recognized (Laungani, 2004). In imperative matters the members of the community arrange meetings and discuss the issues with each other, and any decisions they take are often tied to the members of the community. In the case of mental illness of any family members, it is the responsibility of the individual's family to look after and support him/her. If it gets difficult for family members to look after them, then it is responsibility of the community members to offer support.

Since the individual is an integral part of the family and community, the individual is expected to obey familial and communal norms. Moreover, it is expected that the individual will not deviate from the norms. Pressure of following family norms and fulfilling these expectations creates acute stress in individual members of the family and in some conditions, it leads to psychotic disorders and hysteria (Channabasavanna et al, 1982). Schwartz (1990) describes that collectivism not only gives the social support and feelings of belonging but also it causes anxiety when social obligations are not met. Triandis (2000) writes that there is speculation that extreme individualism and collectivism could be risk factors contributing to poor mental health but no data shows its existence on this topic yet. Weissman (1993) writes that collectivist and traditional cultures could bring about conditions which precipitate depression and anxiety.

Collectivist socialization customs augment dependency and decrease autonomy. Individuals are motivated to treat personal goals as less important, and give importance to group agendas. In addition, he writes that internalizing problems could originate when children get sensitive to parents' high level of control. Externalizing problems are seen as problems of under-control, as children are insufficiently sensitive to social expectations. Diener & Diener (1995) describe that the major disadvantage of collectivist childrearing is that it could weaken the self-esteem of the child, and lead to adults who are compliant but non-innovative, and have lower levels of happiness. Fewer reports of subjective wellbeing in some collectivist cultures could show dissatisfaction with the burden of performing one's duty and the barriers to acquiring self-actualization. The negative result of collectivism shows that being controlled by shame and guilt leads to anxiety about whether one can meet social obligations, and to depression, because shame and guilt interfere with pursuing ones' own goals.

In a collectivistic culture, the individual is seen as interdependent with others and inseparable from the social context. A large number of non-Western collectivistic cultures do not give importance to overt separateness. These cultures place emphasis on the 'fundamental connectedness of human beings.' The major task in these cultures is to maintain connectedness among individuals. Individuals in these cultures are very social and they adjust themselves to the group to which they belong. They want to be sympathetic to, and they play their role for, appropriate actions (Matsumoto, 2004). Therefore, the concept of self-actualization would not fit well therapeutically in a society that does not accept the self as individual. In collectivistic societies, person-centred therapy does not seem to fit.

In Western society, there is emphasis on cognitivism while in Asian culture people believe in emotionalism which is opposite to cognitivism.

Cognitivism is a process in which British people analyse their private and social worlds in specific ways and they shape and support social relationships in it. Pande (1968) writes that British society is considered as a work—and activity-centred society. In this society, individuals emphasize cognition, logic, and control. In this society, it is culturally expected from people in social situations to display self-control in their attitudes and expression of emotions and feelings (Laungani,2004). In the middle classes in Great Britain, display of passions and feelings is frequently disapproved of. It creates mutual discomfort and it is understood as a vulgarity. In Laungani's words, "It is not as though negative feelings and emotions are never expressed, but they are expressed in a subtle way. Even in situations where it would seem legitimate to express feelings openly, the English are guided by control which suggests that one must not cry in public, one must at all times put on a 'brave' face, one must never lose one's dignity. Dignity lies in restraint. If one has to cry, one must do so in the solitude and privacy of one's home, away from prying eyes and ears." (Laungani,

2004:72). Hockey (1993) writes that incapacity of display of emotions and feelings has been a theme that has precipitated some problems to other writers in the discipline.

Time has great importance in work—and activity-centred society. Any sort of work that is not completed on time leaves negative effects on work—and activity-centred society. McClelland (1961) says that dread of passing time, the fear of not to able to achieve short-term and long-term goals on time is considered as a big tension maker in Western society.

According to Laungani (2004) in work—and activity-centred society people want to deal with everything with logic, rationality, and control. A professional therapist or counsellor requires being calm and rational when he/she faces the most tiring conditions in therapy sessions. A counsellor tries to exercise a high degree of control in therapeutic sessions. All this requires the need of the exclusive power of reason. This means one could uncover the nature and structure of reality and knowledge of the external world. In work—and activity-centred society there is a belief that society needs professional therapeutic or counselling settings (Laungani, 2004). In such a society, the objective of person-centred therapy is to make the client able to perceive experience realistically, that emphasizes the rationality. Rogers used the term 'openness to experience' that provides information about capacity for realistic perception. Openness to experience makes the individual's behaviour sufficient and this enables the client to engage in an existential process of living that is a characteristic of rationality (Nelson-Jones, 2001).

Laungani (2004) says that in a relationship-centred society expression of feelings and emotions is not easily suppressed; in general, it is not disapproved of. It can be stated that relationships are managed in a systematic line. In relationship-centred families, crying, depending on others, excessive expressions of emotions, and verbal hostility are not seen as signs of ill-breading or weakness, feelings and emotions, whether they are positive or negative are revealed easily. However, there is a danger of treading incautiously on others' sensibilities and vulnerabilities. Emotional outbursts are considered as symbolic nature—even highly designed and ritualistic. To quarrel, fight, and swear at one another and even from time to time assault one another is frequently common because of closeness of life, a great number of amenities, the absence of privacy etc. These quarrels and outbursts of emotions are of symbolic nature; otherwise, these quarrels could take a form of permanent split, the results of which could be trauma. These outbursts have two forms: at one level, they could be real and at another level, they could be unreal. They play a big role in catharsis.

In hierarchical family structure, each member within a family is aware of his/her own position keeping hierarchy in mind, so, each member learns the normative expression of emotionality to make familial adjustment. Younger members of family do not openly express their negative emotions towards elders because internalized familial norms stop them in doing so. According to Tharp (1991) in societies in which aggression is damped and qualities such as regard and honour are considered important to assure group cohesion, childhood difficulties tend to be for "over controlled" behaviours such as fearfulness and somatisation. In relationship-centred society, the person is completely involved in relationships and he/she follows severe sanctions, which are put on the individual. The person's inability to quit relationships, which have their basis in birth and caste, creates extreme stress and neurosis (Channabasavnna, 1982).

The application of person-centred therapy in relationship-centred society seems to fit well. According to Nelson-Jones(2001) clients, when they visit counsellors for therapy sessions, are helped to express, experience and explore feelings and emotions whether they are positive, negative, ambivalent, or confused. Person-centred therapy is a process in which thoughts and feelings of both the client and his/her therapist are involved. The person-centred therapist provides the attitudinal conditions that take away the emotional deprivations which the client experiences. The therapist provides the right growth-promotional climate and the client becomes less defensive and looks for external regard.

The third cultural difference that distinguishes Western society from Asian culture is that of determinism and free will.

All cultures, the world over, agree with the ideas which are based on free will and determinism (Laungani, 2004). There is a great advancement in the field of science; however, the matters of free will and determinism have not been solved. They have continued emerging in different form of ideas among philosophers such as Schopenhauer, Nietzsche, Heidegger, and Camus (Dilman & Honderich, 1999).

Freud tried to get rid of a tyrannical deterministic model by arguing that these matters have little bearing on the query of free will. It is our 'character' that brings desirable changes to our psyche and accomplishes a powerful rational ego that situates in reality. When someone comes to have a counselling and psychotherapy session, the situation gets a more complicated form. Western therapists seldom make endeavour to get 'solutions' to the difficulties which are presented by clients. Counsellors or therapists clearly say that if clients use their free will, they would be in the position to create the required changes in their psyche, values, passions, attitudes, and their emotions. This type of challenging way of thinking looks at other psychotherapeutic frameworks such as neo-Freudians, behaviourist, and person-centred therapists. To shape our lives, it is emphasized on the determinism but at the personal, social and private level free will demands favour over determinism (Laungani, 2004).

Person-centred therapy can be applied in such a society that is based on free will. In the words of Rogers (1986:127) "In person-centred therapy, the person is free to choose any direction, but actually selects positive and constructive pathways. I can only explain this in terms of a directional tendency inherent in the human organism—a tendency to grow, to develop, to realize its full potential." Rizvi (1989) writes that one of the modes of knowledge Rogers described is the subjective mode of knowledge that includes each person's intentions and sense of freedom. Further, he writes that Rogers places emphasis on each individual's experienced freedom. In Rogers' words (cited in Rizvi, 1989:176) "the experience of choice, of freedom of choice . . . . is not only a profound truth but is a very important element in therapy." Rizvi (1989) describes that Rogers as a scientist was in favour of determinism, but as a therapist he was in favour of freedom.

There is a similar contradiction with regard to the concept of free will and determinism. Indians have the dogma of 'law of karma' while in Pakistani culture there is the belief of 'Amal' (acts, or deeds.) Both the law of Karma and the belief 'Amal' (acts) state that right deeds produce good results and wrong acts produce bad results. Hiriyanna (1949) says that preceding reasons settle happenings of our lives. All actions give their results and the results depend on the nature and kind of actions, therefore, there is decisive justice in the sense that good acts take to pleasure and bad actions to unhappiness.

The belief of 'Amal' or 'Karma' is important because it gives descriptions not only for pain, affliction, and bad luck but also for gratification, joy, and good luck. We get results of our own deeds, not another's. The concept of 'Karma' or 'Amal' emphasizes thatrone's life does not end at death but leads to a new life that is unending. Moral activities of the present life or past life lead to results of a future life that could produce a mechanism of psychological protection in the face of death. This is a belief that will lessen the terror of death and fear of extinction (Laungani, 2004).

The application and scope of person-centred therapy looks less important in Asian culture. The reason could be that in Asian culture especially in the Muslim societies there is a concept of Amal (acts)—good deeds produce good results and wrong deeds produce bad results. In such a society or culture that is totally based on the belief of Amal and concept of pre-determined fate, person-centred therapy does not seem to be appropriate for counselling of people who have this belief. The major reason is that such societies are based on spiritualism in which every act whether it is good or wrong is viewed from a religious perspective. In these societies, it is a belief that closeness to God is a sign of good physical and mental health (Rizvi, 1989). In these societies, individuals worship God, perform religious rites, recite the Quran (Holy Book) and contact religious scholars to get forgiveness from God for their sins. In this situation, if they contact any psychotherapists or counsellors they do not feel satisfaction. Therefore, they think that they had better communicate with religious scholars to remove their guilt feelings. According to Rizvi(1989) in Muslim societies the Murshid (religious scholar, or in modern words spiritual counsellor or therapist) has great importance in developing a relationship between the client and himself. For this purpose, a normal individual spiritual psychology was evolved.

The fourth cultural difference between Asian society and Western society is materialism and spiritualism. In Asian society, people emphasize spirituality. In the concept of spiritualism, they believe in self and perfectionism, which are considered important parts of human personality.

Materialism is a belief that world is composed of matter. There is a hackneyed myth that all explanations of phenomena, ranging from lunar cycles to lunacy, need to be sought within the (assumed) materialist frame work. Psychiatrists, medical practitioners, and psychologists show reluctance to deal with any explanations, which are of a non-material or supernatural nature. Non-material explanations of supernatural ESP, evil spirits, ghosts, and other supernatural 'forces' are dealt with scepticism and at worst with scorn (Laungani et al, 1999).

The philosophy of materialism is that our knowledge of the world is external to ourselves; reality is as it were. It is an objective scientific venture that one would accomplish knowledge of the external world and grasp reality as well. Those psychiatrists and psychologists who express their desire to conceive alternative non-material descriptions are in a small minority. They are aware of the fact that anyone who presents such explanations of phenomena is in danger of sustaining the displeasure of the scientific community. Non-material descriptions or superstitious and backward societies are seen in underdeveloped countries (Launagani et al, 1999). Arkin (2002) writes that Western societies are more secular, therefore suggesting that materialism is increasing. Merton (1968) wrote that materialism is prevalent in societies where wealth and status are depicted as attainable for everyone in society. If in a culture money plays a major role in achievements, and emphases on the individual are considered important then it will show that people establish extrinsic aspirations, especially in the pursuit of assets, financial gains, and social recognition in respect of these goals (Kasser, 1993). Yankelovich (1981) says that materialistic societies have created selfishness and egoistic tendencies. Western capitalist societies give emphasis to individuality and competition.

Bynner (1998) describes that British children have been socialized because they are taught to rely on and trust in themselves; as a result they are selfish and materialistic. Livingstone (1998) stated that culturally Britain is more individualistic than the rest of Europe. Rudmin (1992) says that materialistic people might have more chances to follow a highly complex material life and they can less relate themselves to environment. Belk (1988) writes that a high level of materialistic thinking could be related to low levels of self-esteem and depression that show poor psychological well being. Kasser (2001) writes that people who have powerful materialistic values will show or have lower self-esteem. In addition, he says that people who give priority to money, popularity, and beauty are more inclined to depression; they have behavioural problems and a low level of self-actualization. The application of person-centred therapy seems to be very useful in a materialistic society in which people have a low level of self-actualization. The main emphasis of the therapy is to make clients acquire their proper self-actualization.

In Asian culture, materialism is considered an unimportant concept. Beliefs and values of Asians are linked to spiritualism. For Asian people, the external world is not composed of matter but is seen as being illusory. In their views, reality and its perception exist within the individual. They say the main and ultimate objective of human existence is to surpass one's illusory physical existence, give up the world of material aspiration and get a heightened state of spiritual awareness (Radhakerishnan, 1989). The supreme concern of the Asian mind is to discover the self (Sinari, 1984). Inward seeking spiritual consciousness cannot be achieved overnight. For this meditative perspective the individual needs to make continued efforts. Everything individuals know about themselves and express is subject to variation and decay. But the acquisition of the self, as Zimmer (cited in Laungani, 2004) says, is forever changeless, beyond time and space, and even beyond the normal (scientific) methods of human understanding. It exceeds mental and logical understanding. Hence, the major objective of Asian philosophy is to know and understand this self that leads to a complete transformation of the individual: a transmutation of the soul. The major goal of this philosophy is to create a basic change in human nature, a change that at least leads to human perfection, a divine God-like state (Laungani, 2004). According to Zimmer (1989), this makes Asians more inward looking and Westerners more outward looking. Rizvi (1989) writes that spiritual endeavours are such ways through which man can cleanse his/her soul and achieve higher states of being. In brief, he/she could be a perfect person.

Kakar(1982) writes that mental illness in Asians could be described in terms of magic, and by the possession of one's soul by evil and malevolent forces. Their belief in magical explanations is widespread, and there are a number of people who are specially qualified to understand the activities of evil spirits. In the case of serious and sudden ailment within a family, such 'experts' are called by the family members to expel the spells, cast out the effects of 'evil eyes', undo the malignity of magic, take on religious ceremonies to counteract the negative influence of ominous events, etc. in order to help the afflicted person to recover (Kakar, 1982). Rizvi (1989) writes that Muslim thinkers removed the magic method and gave the scientific outlook of psychotherapy. Ibn Miskwayh, cited in Rizvi (1989) classifies the spiritual disorders. He described passions and emotions. He says that anger is a mental state that could precipitate mental disequilibrium. Excessive anger moves the social and personal life of the individual to a miserable condition, in which the person avoids joining the company of others and starts feeling loneliness. This leads him/her to gloom and depression.

In a society that emphasizes spiritualism, the Alim (religious scholar) provides his services as a counsellor or therapist for the treatment of mental disorders. Laungani (2004) writes that in such a society it is believed that stress, distress, and afflictions are calamity from God. People, in such societies, take the afflicted individual to a well-known temple, shrine, or mosque where they meet a well-known Alim, who has divine healing powers. The Alim suggests the person say prayers five times a day regularly, perform religious rites, recite the Quran everyday. The emphasis is on establishing a relationship between the Alim and the follower (Sinha , 1990). The therapeutic procedure between the follower and the Alim takes a directive approach rather than a non-directive one. In this procedure, the follower is asked to abide by all teachings and prescriptions of the Alim.

For therapeutic progress, it is important for the Alim to be recognized as an individual of enormous wisdom. The follower is expected to say prayers, perform religious rites, and to fast. All this is done in the belief that the victim will recover his/her mental and physical health (Laungani, 2004).

Confessionism is a firmly established cultural practice in the West in which there is a declaration, and acknowledgment or admission of a fault, weakness or crime. In confession it is expected from persons to disclose his/her actions and secret feelings or opinion. In confession, there is need for someone who, as an audience, listens, considers, judges, and punishes and could receive and forgive as he/she reflects back to us who we are. In confession, a person displays his/her identity (Besley, 2005). There are different kinds of confession. In religion, the form of confession is to make a verbal acknowledgement of perpetrating a sin. In the sense of literature 'confession' consists of components of recognizing the self in a detailed, self conscious attempt to displaying and demonstrating oneself to an audience. Counselling is a secular process that firmly establishes cultural practices, which are related to the self, such as care of the self, self-knowledge, and confession. The professional counselling relationship provides the opportunity to confess with the assurance that the counsellor is bound by ethical conventions of confidentiality. Counsellors need to understand the historical and philosophical contexts in which cultural practices keep their existence and which are helpful to investigate the genealogy of the confessional self.

"'Why truth'—and why must the care of the self occur only through the concern for truth? [This is] the question for the West. How did it come about that all of Western culture began to revolve around this obligation of truth—?" (Foucault, 1997, cited in Besley, 2005: 369).

In Asian culture there is an emphasis on Tawbah; especially religious-minded people like to pass through this process to get forgiveness from God for their sins or wrong works they perpetrate.

To tell the truth is considered very important and valuable in Western society. In present Western society, expressing oneself truly rather than keeping secrets is de rigueur. For example, on TV shows people publicly make confessions of their stories of physical, sexual and emotional abuse; alcoholism and drug use; sexual practices, affairs, harassment. A large number of people visit a therapist or counsellor for their personal problems. The process of confession with the passage of time has increasingly changed. In the Western world, the effects of Christianity cannot be underrated even though a great number of people might follow a more secular kind of life. Mainly in religious contexts, sins related to sexual morality need to be confessed. As a result, religious confession took the form of a principal technology to manage the sexual lives of followers, by making the confession of the 'truth' about one's sexual thoughts and behaviours. Up to the 16th century confession was performed in church but after the Reformation, individuals not only started making confession of his/her acts but also thoughts (Besley, 2005). Foucault (1980:215) says that the 18th century saw 'brutal' medical techniques emerging which consists in simply demanding that the subject tells his or her story, or narrate it in writing. Confession is an autobiographical process that urges the individual to recreate him/herself. People can get assistance in this by seeking out varieties of therapeutic procedures such as counselling. In Besely's (2005) views "In secular society, therapeutic forms of confession, where the psychotherapists or counsellors could be considered akin to the priest, have replaced the theological form. Although the use of listening techniques and the uncovering of 'self' are similar, the elements of advice, admonition and punishment that are involved in the religious forms of confession are certainly no part of contemporary counselling—a practice predicted on the assumption that the client is telling the truth about him/herself i.e. disclosure in therapy/counselling.

Counsellors should be aware of the role they perform in use of techniques. Moreover, they should concentrate on becoming more conscious about providing a means to address care of the self of which confession forms only a part. In this way, counselling could employ understandings of philosophy to give a practical component, "A way of life, of being and a search for wisdom that transforms the self and which develops self-mastery (Besley, 2005: 380).

According to Rogers (1951), the counsellor's objective in a therapy session is to explore the attitude and problems clients experience but deny having in their awareness. The result of the verbal exploration of attitudes and problems is called 'the discovery of the attitudes'. Clients usually talk about "things I had never previously thought of." The most significant phenomena of therapy are to discover the client's emotions and attitudes that they do not recognize consciously. Rogers (1951:77) writes about the experience of a veteran in therapy session in simple terms: "During counselling, he was forced, in his own mind to admit that several of these things were wrong. He began to think and actually admit things to himself about himself that he had never considered admitting before. He began to see just what was at the root of all his actions. Why he was so often apt to cover up what he had done with excuses."

Person-centred therapy is related to individual self, such as care of the self, self-knowledge, and confession. The professional counselling relationship provides the opportunity to confess with the assurance that the counsellor is bound by ethical conventions of confidentiality.

The concept of Tawbah (Repentance) has been derived from the Quran and Hadith (the words of the Holy Prophet Mohammed), and it provides the stamp of divinity and authenticity to the act of confession as a therapeutic measure (Rizvi,1989). According to Rizvi(1989) Tawbah is the remedy to eradicate evil. It is a contract for the future. Tawbah gives meaning and understanding of the wrongness of an act when the individual perpetrates the act. It is his/

her determination not to do the act again. Further he writes that a large number of Muslim therapists say that people are guilt-conscious and they realize that it is too late for them to expect forgiveness, and this causes mental disorders. Troubled and afflicted, with the sense of terror of their own wickedness, they are also afraid that their trouble would pass away and that they might lose their sense of guilt without remission of their sins. They live in a condition of depression for years. Nothing holds their mind but denunciation, and the expectation of damnation. Later, infrequently, they enjoy periods of peace when they pursue comforting texts from the Holy Quran and Hadith, concerning the importance of Tawbah. Such a period is prolonged until the verses of the Quran convince them that their sin is not unforgivable and the period of depression by and large ends, once the fact that salvation through goodness is known to them.

Prominent Muslim thinkers state that on the spiritual level the importance of confession exists in the fact that it maintains a healthy attitude to sin and provides a basic cure for it. The act of confession deals both with the personal and psychic welfare of individuals. The suffering could carry on afflicting an individual, even though the legal arm of society might never punish him/her. He/she feels him/herself unworthy and feels that he/she is not able to make any contribution to society. A mentally disturbed individual could not sense this alienation, but this flaw is because of lack of socialization that he/she does not feel any guilt and does not recognise from wrong, sin from virtue (Rizvi, 1989).

The concept of Tawbah offers the suffering individual a hope of forgiveness. Forgiveness is the pre-requisite and without it, the procedure of rapprochement between the patient and the world and God cannot occur. Forgiveness gives hope to the sinner to re-establish the relationship with God and his neighbour, instead of carrying on as a hopeless victim of retaliation or alienation. Tawbah consists of three parts: contrition, confession, and satisfaction. Real sorrow for perpetrating some misgiving is an important starting point on the road to retrieval of interpersonal relationships. Confession is a process to share with God and a symbolic representative of the community, the nature and importance of one's sins, with a sense of ethical responsibility. The dynamics of confession is known as 'catharsis' in psychotherapy. Confession is highly structured. Judgement does not get suspension, since patient and confessor stand under the judgement of God. Guilt and responsibility are neither sidestepped nor brushed off, but are received as realities. Repentance and confession of sins are essential for forgiveness (Rizvi, 1989).

Confession and Tawbah introduce a variation in the old patterns of life, therefore, it affects soul, mind, and body. The complete personality of an individual is involved in it. This fact appears in modern times too. Robert H. Thuless (cited in Rizvi, 1989:37) writes, "Private confession is helpful in many instances. My experience indicates that confession is therapeutically helpful, as well as theologically and sacramentally. I have counselled successfully as a priest, when trained psychologists have failed. It is amazing how some patients respond to the therapy of grace, which provided when other methods failed. The fact of divine aid has tremendous psychological effect. The removal of guilt is in fact efficacious, where there is real sorrow, because of a supernatural motive and a sincere intention of amendment."

Person-centred therapy does not seem to fit well when an individual is religious-minded in Asian culture. Tawbah is a form of counselling. It can be called a religious counselling in which a sinner raises his/her hands in prayer to get forgiveness from God. After Tawbah the individual feels peace and satisfaction. As Rizvi (1989) writes, Tawbah is the annihilation of all savageries. The individual surrenders completely to the will of God. Repentance is very important for people whenever they perform wrong acts. They had better turn to God in repentance. "God pardons him unto who turns to Him with a pertinent heart." By repentance, one becomes the beloved of God. Therefore, it is essential for a normal person to be close to God and to get full knowledge of Him, and comply with His commands whole-heartedly.

The next chapter (Chapter Five) will give conclusions and recommendations which would be helpful for future study in the area of cultural psychology.

CHAPTER FIVE

CONCLUSION AND RECOMMENDATIONS

This chapter contains the conclusion and recommendations after a review of person-centred therapy, aims and objectives of the research, comparison of counselling courses, and cultural differences and problems people face, for which they visit counsellors or psychotherapists for removal of their problems.

The study, after exploration of cultural differences and a comparison of counselling courses, concludes that culture has powerful influences on a person's identity and personality. Cultural norms help in initiating, sustaining, and controlling the private, familial, and social behaviour of individuals. British culture gives importance to individualism that creates an atmosphere of competition and a high level of creativity. In this culture personal responsibility and self-achievement have great importance. People in this society like to live in a nuclear family system. Social behaviour is called 'class related'. In this society emphasis is given to identity. As Laungani (2004) says, in Western culture identity is seen in socio-cognitive developmental term. In such a society anxiety is related to acquisition of identity. Erikson (1963) writes that acquiring a proper identity is very difficult. Non-fulfilment of identity leads to stress, and loneliness. In such a society, person-centred therapy is best to use because in this society self-individual is emphasized. Person-centred therapy works to release the blockage of self-actualization (Nelson-Jones, 2001).

Pakistani culture is an entirely different culture from British culture. In this culture, people like to be collectively attached to each other. Pakistani society is purely a relationship-centred society in which relationship with others is given much importance. According to Hui & Triandis (1986) collectivistic cultures perform a great role in making personal relationships strong. In this society people emphasize collective personality and collective achievement. Social behaviour is based on caste and religion in this society. Religion plays a major role in lives of people in this society and reflection of religious rituals appear in day-to-day behaviours. Anxiety and other problems are related to a caste and a familial related identity. In this society collectivism creates dependency that leads to depression and anxiety. This society is based on social support and belongingness. Deprivation of social support and belongingness becomes a cause of psychological problems. In this society there is an emphasis on connectedness among people therefore person-centred therapy cannot be applied.

The main cultural difference, in the researcher's view, that distinguishes British culture from Pakistani culture is that of free will and determinism. In British society, there is an emphasis on individual freedom while in Pakistani culture individual freedom has less importance that precipitates many psychological problems. In British society freedom of choice is emphasized. In this society, success or failure are considered a part of effort. Self-blame or guilt is considered a residual result of failure. In this society person-centred therapy is very useful. Rogers (1987) writes that in therapy sessions the client is free to choose any direction in positive and constructive ways.

In Pakistani culture, there is less freedom of choice. In this society people have a belief in Amal (acts) and pre-determined fate. Success or failure is related to one's Amal (deeds) but effort is considered very important for achieving success. In the condition of failure, no guilt is related to failure because people in this society believe in luck and bad luck. Such a society is mainly based on religion, and people in this society believe in spiritualism. In this society people visit religious scholars when they commit any bad deeds therefore the religious scholar takes the form of a counsellor. In this society person-centred therapy cannot be applied because people believe in luck and bad luck. People believe in pre-determined fate.

The study of confession and Tawbah leads to the conclusion that it is another great difference that distinguishes British culture from Pakistani culture. Confession is recognized as a cultural practice in British society. In this society people not only make confession of their acts but also they make confession of what they say. Besley (2005) writes that during 16th century people went to church for their confession, and after Reformation they liked to make confession of their thoughts. The most interesting point that distinguishes British people from Pakistanis is to make confession in writing. Foucault (1980) writes that since 18th century people like to tell their stories in writing. In Pakistani culture it seldom occurs that people make their confession in writing. Person-centred therapy is related to self-confession therefore it can be used in British culture.

In Pakistani culture people have a belief that if they perpetrate any wrong act and in result they are guilt-conscious then Tawbah is the only way to escape from God's punishment. As Rizvi (1989) writes, Tawbah is the remedy to eradicate evils. As Pakistani people give importance to spiritualism, they believe that confession exists on a spiritual level. The process of confession on a spiritual level gives them personal and psychic welfare. Rizvi (1989) describes that Tawbah is the stamp of divinity and authenticity to the act of confession. Tawbah is a process to get forgiveness from God. Forgiveness gives hope to a sinner that he/she is able to re-establish relation with God. This process takes the individual close to God. As Maulana Ashraf Ali Thanvi (cited in Rizvi, 1989) writes, remoteness from God creates mental disorders. Tawbah can be called a religious counselling. For Tawbah no one needs just individual raises his/her hands to God for forgiveness. In such a society Person-centred therapy cannot be applied because in Pakistani culture people like spiritualism, that is why people prefer contacting spiritual healers to visiting counsellors or therapists for removal of their psychological problems.

Furthermore, comparison of counselling courses leads to the conclusion that in Pakistan counselling needs the attention of psychologists and counselling psychologists for its professional establishment. Conclusion of counselling courses leads to the following recommendations:

Counselling psychology needs to be taught as a compulsory subject in MSc courses of psychology at universities. Furthermore, a specific Master's degree should be issued by universities in Pakistan. At universities counselling psychologists and counsellors need to be appointed to give training in counselling therapies and tests. Research methods should be part of counselling courses.

Counselling training centres need to be established in the main cities of Pakistan so that professional counsellors could be provided.

REFERENCES

Almas, I. & Ibrahim, F. A. (1983) School Counselling in Pakistan. International Journal for the Advancement of Counselling; 6 (2): 93-98.

Almas, I. & Ibrahim, F. A. (1985) Preparation of Counsellors in Pakistan: A Proposed Model. International Journal for the Advancement of Counselling; 8 (4):323-327.

Arkin, R. M. & Linchiat, C.(2002) Materialism as an attempt to cope with uncertainty. Psychology and Marketing; 19 (5): 389-406.

Axelson, J. A. (1999) Counselling and Development in a Multicultural Society. London; Brooks/Cole Publishing Company.

Bergin, A and Garfield, S. (1991) Handbook of Psychotherapy and Behaviour Change: John Willey.

Besley, C. A. (2005) Self-denial or self-mastery? Foucault's genealogy of the confessional self. British Journal of Guidance & Counselling; 33 (3): 365-380.

Brown, P. & Abel Smith, A.(1996). 'Psychological counselling in mid-life issues', in R. Woolfe & W. Dryden (eds), Handbook of counselling Psychology. London: Sage.

Burks, H. M. & Stefflre, B. (1979) Theories of counselling 3rd Ed. New York: McGraw-Hill.

Burnham, J. B. (1986) Family Therapy. London: Routledge.

Bynner, J. (1998) Materialism Rules for British Teens (The Sunday Times 8th March, 1998 p.4).

Carrithers, M. (1992) Why Humans Have Culture: Explaining Anthropology and Social Diversity. Oxford: Oxford University Press.

Carter, E.A. & McGoldrick, M. (1980) The Family Life Cycle. London: Gardner Press.

Channabasavanna, S. M. & Bhatti, R. S. (1982) A study on interactional patterns of family typologies in families of mental patients, in A. Kiev and V. Rao (eds) Readings in Transcultural Psychiatry, 149-61. Madras: Higginsbothams.

Clarke, T. P.(1994) Stress management And Counselling: A person-centred approach to Stress management. British Journal of guidance and counselling; 22 (1): 27-37.

Cohen, D. & Nisbett, R. E. (1994) Self-protection and the culture of honor. Explaining southern violence. Personality and Social Psychology Bulletin, 20, 551-567.

Corney, R. (1992) 'Studies of the effectiveness of counselling in general practice', in R. Corney and R. Jenkins (eds), counselling in General Practice. London: Routledge.

Corney, R. & Jenkins, R. (1992) Counselling in General Practice. London:Routledge.

Cross, W. E. (1971) 'The negro-to-black conversion-experience: toward a psychology of Black liberation', Black World, 20:13-27.

D` Ardenne, P. & Mahtani, A.(1989) Transcultural Counselling in action. London: Sage.

Davidson, A. R., Jaccard, J. J., Triandis, H. C., Morales, M. L. & Diaz-Guerrero, R (1976) Cross-cultural model testing: Toward the solution of the etic-emic dilemma. International Journal of Psychology, 11, 1-13.

Davy, J. & Ellis, S. (2000) Counselling Skills in Palliative Care. Buckingham: Open University Press.

Diener, E. & Diener, M. B. (1995) Cross-cultural correlates of life satisfaction and self-esteem. Journal of Personality and Social Psychology, 68, 653-663.

Farhat, N. (2007) Personal Communication.

Erickson, E. H. (1968) Identity, Youth and Crisis. New York: Faber & Faber.

Farber, B. A. & Heifetz, L. J. (1982) The process and dimensions of burnout in psychotherapists. Professional Psychology, 13, 293-301.

Farber, B. A. (1983a) Stress and Burnout in the Human Service Professions. New York: Pergamon.

Freud, S. (1962) Civilization and its Discontents. New York: W. W. Norton.

Geiser, C. (1997) Taking the risk of being fully alive— personal comments on working and training on the small edge between doing and being. Vortrag an der IVth International conference on Client-Centred and Experiential Psychotherapy, Lissabon, July.

Goldberg, D. & Huxley, P. (1992) Common Mental Disorders. London: Routledge.

Gul, A. & Mubeen, S. et al (2003) What probably made a difference? A Qualitative Study of Anxious and Depressed women who exhibited Different Levels of Change after counselling. Journal of Pakistan Medical Association; 53 (6): 1-6.

Hiriyanna, M. (1949) The Essentials of Indian Philosophy. London: Allen & Unwin.

Hoare, C. H.(1991) Psychological identity development and cultural others. Journal of Counselling and Development; 70: 45-53.

Hockey, J. (1993) The acceptable face of human grieving? The clergy's role in managing emotional expression during funerals, in D. Clark (ed) The Sociology of Death, pp. 129-48. Oxford: Blackwell.

Hofstede, G. (2001).Culture's Consequences (2nd edition). London: Sage.

Hui, C. H. & Triandis, H. C.(1986) Individualism-collectivism: A study of cross-cultural researchers. Journal of cross-cultural Psychology, 17, 225-248.

Illahi, N. (1988) Psychotherapy services to the ethnic communities, report of a study Ealing Hospital, London. Unpublished paper.

Jabeen, S. (2007) Personal Communication.

Kakar, S. (1992) Identity and Adulthood. Delhi: Oxford India Paperbacks.

Kakar, S. (1982) Shamans, Mystics and Doctors. London: Mandala Books.

Kasser, T. & Ryan, R. M. (1993) A dark side of the American dream: correlates of financial success as a central life aspiration. Journal of personality and social psychology; 65, 410-422.

Kasser, T. & Kasser, V.G. (2001) The dreams of people high and low in Materialism. Journal of economic Psychology; 22 (6) 693-719.

Keleman, Stanley. (1986) Bonding: A Somatic-Emotional Approach to Transference, Center Press.

Kitayama, S. Markus, H. R. & Norasakkunity (1997) Individual and collective process in the construction of the self: self-enhancement in the United States and self-criticism in Japan. Journal of Personality and Social Psychology, 72 (6): 1245-67.

Laungani, P. & Palmer, S. (eds) (1999) Counselling in a multicultural society. London: Sage.

Laungani, P. (2004) Asian perspectives in counselling and psychotherapy. Hove: Brunner/Routledge

Layard, R. (2005) Happiness: Lessons from a new science. London: Allen Lane.

Levine, R. A. (1973) Culture, Behaviour and Personality. Chicago: Aldine.

Livingstone (1998) Materialism as an attempt to cope with uncertainty. Psychology and Marketing; 19 (15): 389-406.

Lsatuke, K. (2005) Temporal patterns of improvement in client-centred therapy And Cognitive –behaviour therapy. British Journal of Counselling Psychology; 18(2): 95—108.

Maslach, C. & Jackson, S. E. (1984) Burnout in organisational settings. In S. Oskamp (ed.) Applied Social Psychology Annual 5: Application in Organizational Settings. London: Sage.

Masson, J. (1989) Against Therapy. London: Collins.

Matsumoto, D., & Juang, L. (2004) Culture And Psychology (3rd edition). London: Wadsworth Thomson Learning, Inc.

McLeod, J. & Daniel, T (2006) Weighing up the evidence: A qualitative analysis of how Person-client centred counsellors evaluate the effectiveness of their practice. British Journal of Counselling and Psychotherapy Research; 6 (4):244-249.

Merry, T. (2002).Learning and Being in Person-Centred Counselling (2nd edition).Ross-on-Wye: PCCS Books.

Merton, R. K. (1968) Social theory and social structure. New York: Free Press.

Muynuck de, A. & Moran, B. M. (1999) A randomised trial of the impact of counselling on treatment adherence of tuberculosis patients in Sialkot, Pakistan. Int J Tuberc Lung Dis ; 3 (12): 1073-1080.

Nelson-Jones, N. R. (2001) Theory and Practice of Counselling & Therapy (3rd edition). London: Sage.

Parekh, B. (2000) Rethinking Multiculturalism: Cultural Diversity and Political Theory. Basingstoke: Macmillan/ Palgrave.

Pedersen, P. (1987) Handbook of Cross-cultural Counselling and Therapy. London: Praeger Publisher.

Radhakrishnan, S. (1989) Indian Philosophy, vol.2 (centenary edition). Delhi: Oxford Univeristy Press.

Rahman, S. & Khandwalla, H. E. (2000) Knowledge, attitudes, and practices regarding sexually transmitted infections among general practitioners and medical specialists in Karachi, Pakistan. Sexually Transmitted Infections; 76: 383-385.

Rizivi, S. A. A. (1989) Muslim Tradition in Psychotherapy & Modern Trends. Lahore: Institute of Islamic Culture.

Rogers, C. R. (1951) Client –Centred Therapy: Its Current Practice, Implications and Theory. London: Constable & Robinson Ltd.

Rogers, C. R. (1986a) Rogers, Kohut, and Erickson. Person-Centred Review, 1(2):125-40.

Rogers, C. R. (1982) Client Centred Therapy. London: Constable Publishing Co.

Rudmin & Kibourne (1992) Materialism and economic psychology. Journal of economic Psychology; 15, 217-231.

Russell, J. (1999) counselling and the social construction of self. British Journal of Guidance and Counselling; 27 (3): 339-351.

Schwartz, H. S. (1990) Individualism—Collectivism critique and proposed refinements. Journal of Cross-cultural Psychology, 21, 139-157.

Scully, R. (1983) The work-settings support group: a means of preventing burnout. In B. A Farber (ed.) Stress and Burnout in the Human Service Professions. New York: Pergamon.

Sharma, A. (2000) Classical Hindu Thought: An Introduction. New Delhi: Oxford University Press.

Sinari, R. A. (1984) The Structure of Indian Thought. Delhi: Oxford University Press.

Sinha, J. B. P. & Sinha, D. (1990) Role of social values in Indian organization, Journal of Transpersonal Psychology, 12(2): 127-42.

Steven, M. J., & Wedding, D. (2004). Handbook of International Psychology. New York: Brunner-Routledge Publisher.

Sue, D. W. Sue, D. (1999) Counselling the culturally different (3d edition). New York: John Wiley.

Sue, D.W. (1981) Evaluation process variables in cross-cultural counselling and psychotherapy , in A.J. Marsella and P.B. Pedersen (eds), Cross-Cultural Counselling and Psychotherapy. New York: Pergamon.

Tharp, R. G. (1991) Cultural diversity and treatment of children. Journal of Counselling and Clinical Psychology, 59, 799-812.

Thorne, B. (2003) Carl Rogers (2nd edition). London: Sage.

Thorne, B. (1992) Carl Rogers. London: Sage.

Thorne, B. Mearns, D. (1988). Person –centred counselling in Action. London: Sage.

Triandis, H. C.(2000) Cultural Syndromes and subjective well-being. In E. F. Diener & E. M. Suh (Eds), Subjective well-being across cultures (pp.87-112). Cambridge, MA: MIT Press.

Triandis, H.D., & Gelfand, M.J. (1998) Converging measurement of horizontal and vertical individualism and collectivism. Journal of Personality and Social Psychology, 74, 118-128.

Triandis, H. (1980) Introduction, in H.C. Triandis and J. W. Berry (eds) Handbook of cross—cultural Psychology, vol. 2, Boston, MA: Allyn & Bacon.

Van Belle, H. (1980) Basic Intent and Therapeutic Approach of Carl Rogers. Toronto:Wedge Publishing Foundation.

Vitz, P. (1994) Psychology as a religion: the Cult of self-worship. Grand Rapids, MI: William B. Eerdmans.

Watson, N. (1984) 'The empirical staus of Rogers's hypotheses of the necessary and sufficient conditions for effective psychotherapy', in R.F. Levant and J.M. Shlien (eds), Client-Centred Therapy and the Person-centred Approach. New York: Praeger. pp 17-40.

Warnath, C. F. & Shelton, J. L. (1976) The ultimate disappointment: the burned-out counsellor. Personnel and Guidance Journal, 55, 172-5.

Weissman, J. R. (1993) Parent reports of behavioural and emotional Problems among children in Kenya, Thailand and the United States. Child development, 64, 98-109.

Yankelovich, (1981) Materialism: Trait Aspects of living in the material world. Journal of consumer Research; 12, 265-280.

Zimmer, H. (1989) Philosophies of India (Bollingen Series XXV1). Princeton, NJ: Princeton University Press.

www.ingramcontent.com/pod-product-compliance
Lightning Source LLC
Chambersburg PA
CBHW050358290526

45786CB00003B/1035